DISCOVER SERIES
CIENCIA

Átomo

Bebe con microscopio

Viales de sangre

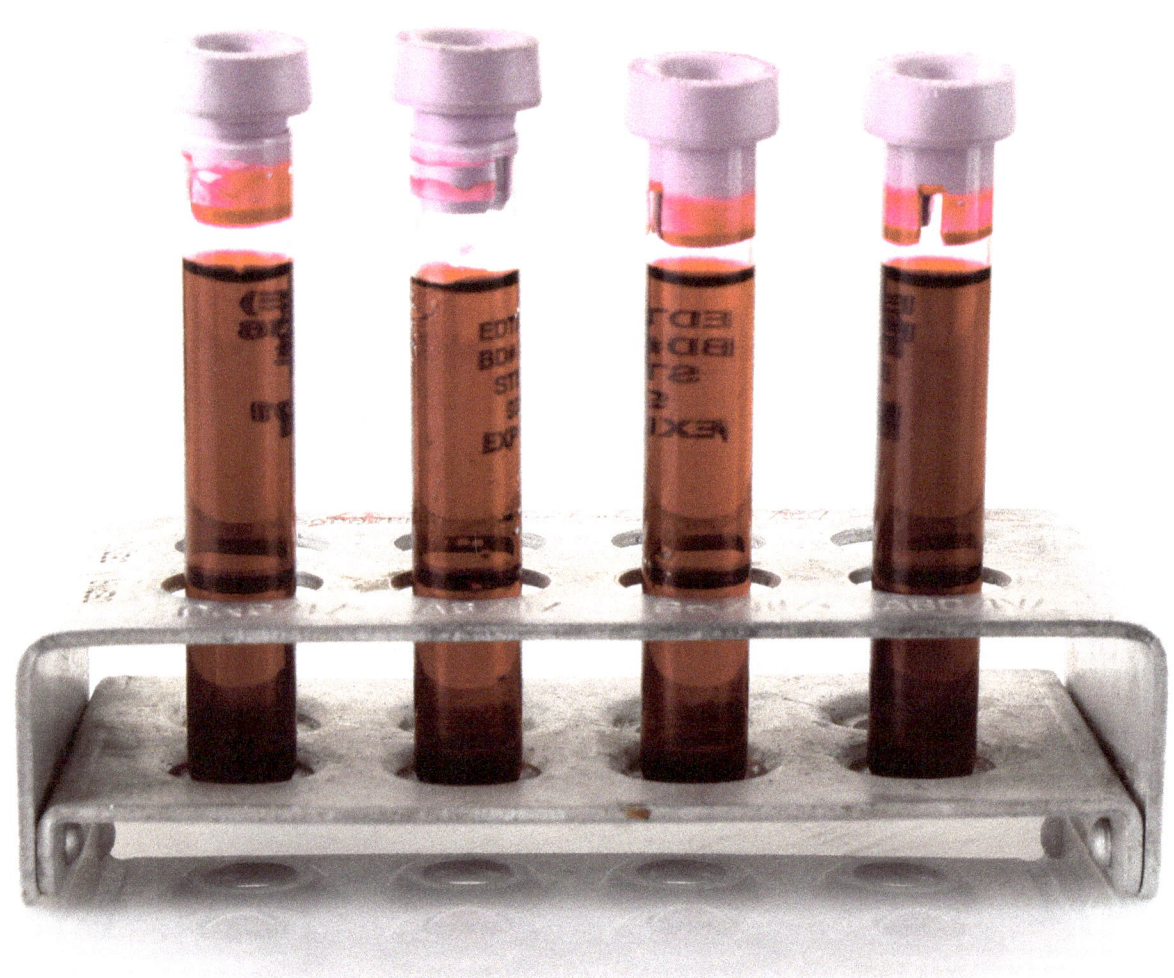

Mechero Bunsen

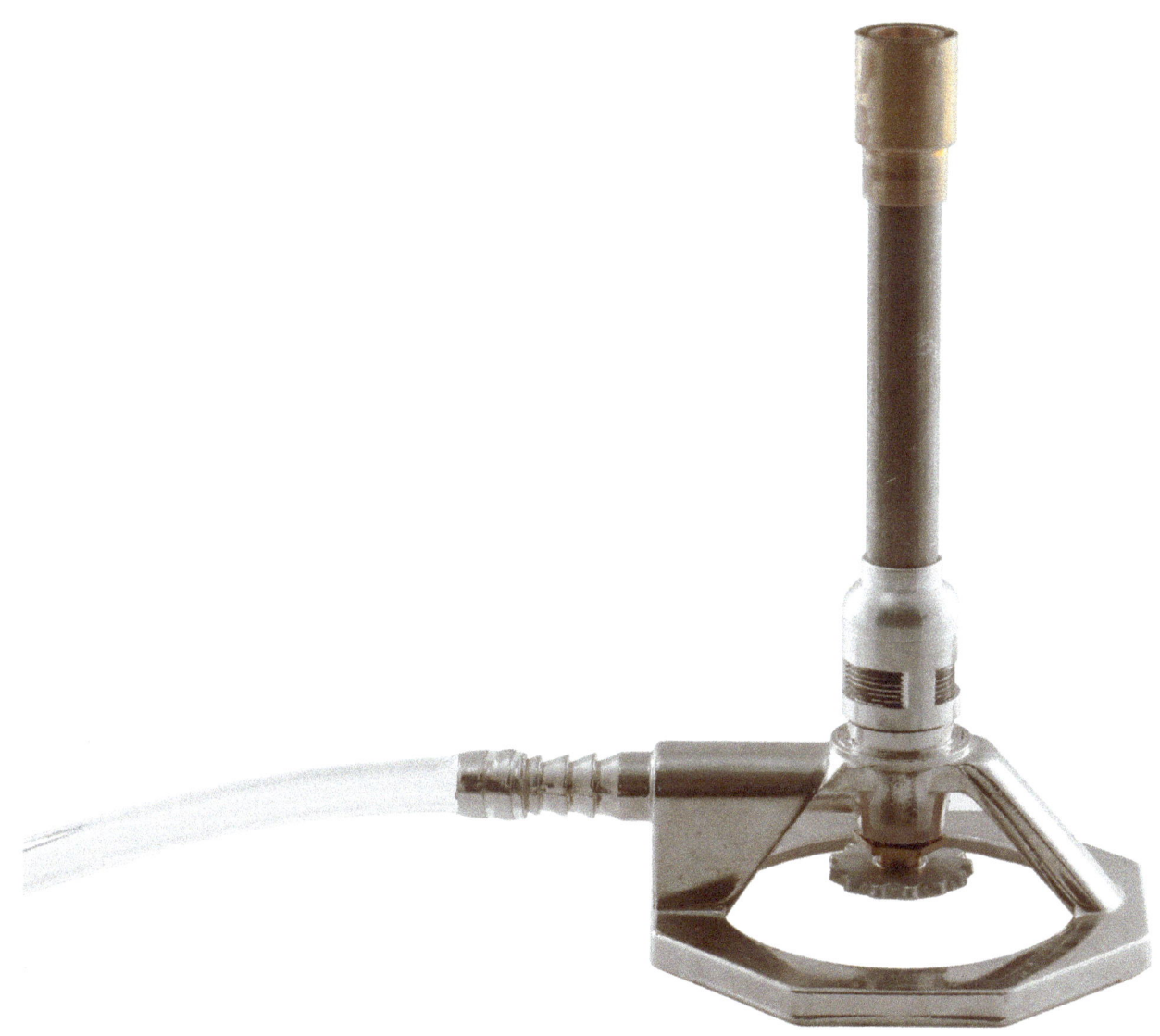

ADN

Matraz Erlenmeyer (matraz cónico)

Cámara de goteo intravenosa

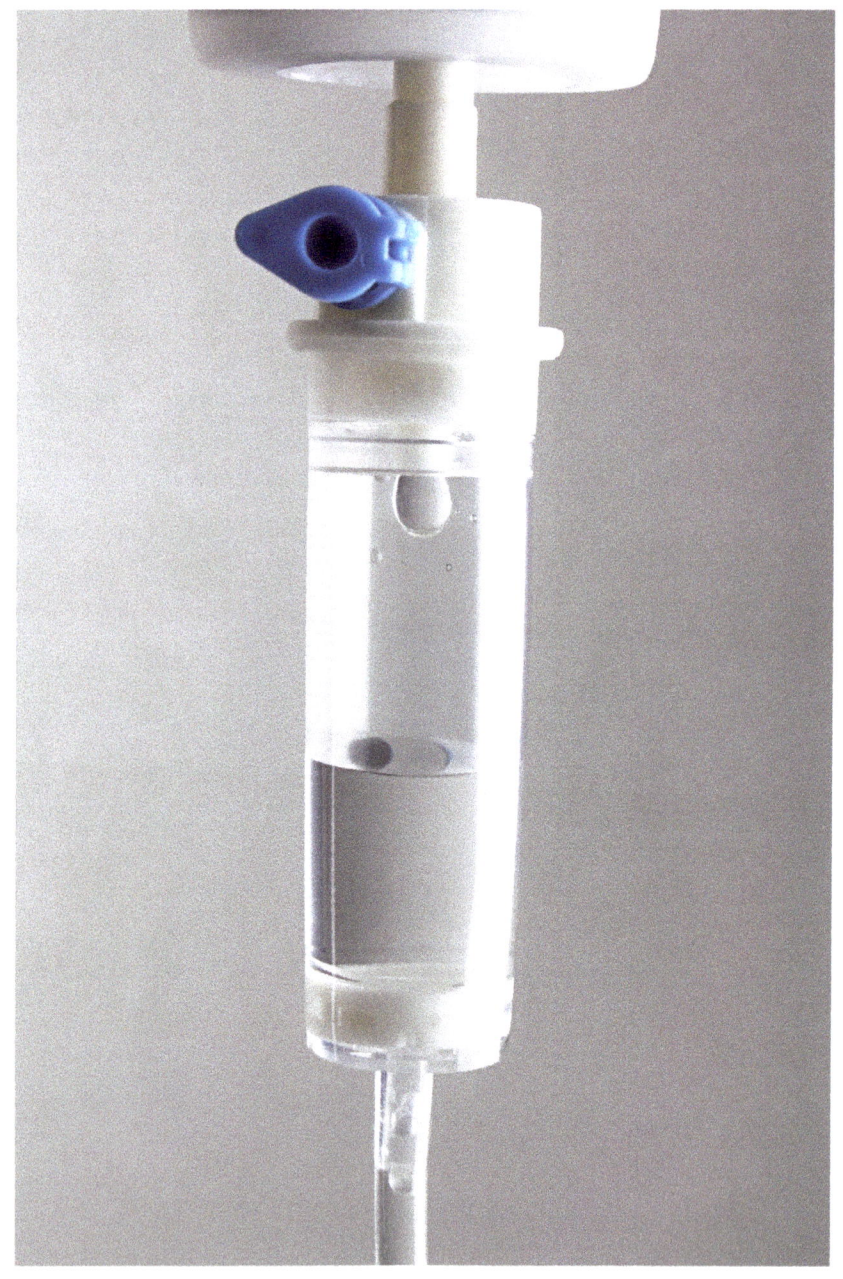

Cristaleria de laboratorio

Microscopio professional de laboratorio

Rata de laboratorio

Laboratorio

Imán

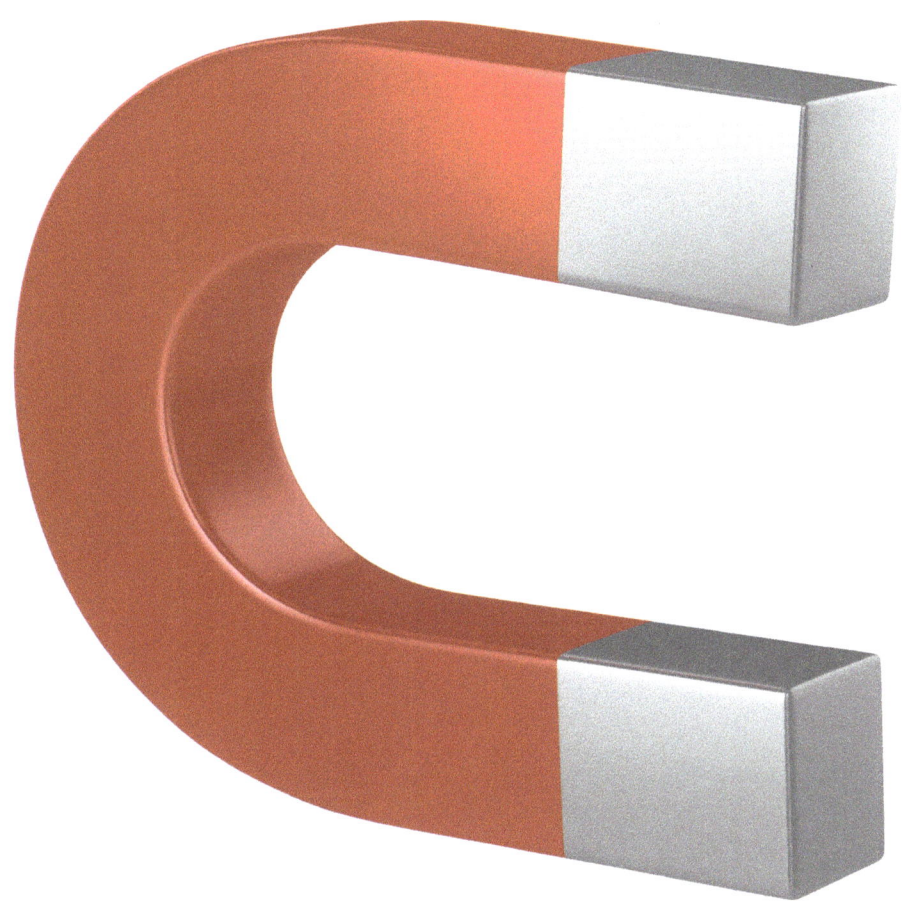

Microscopio

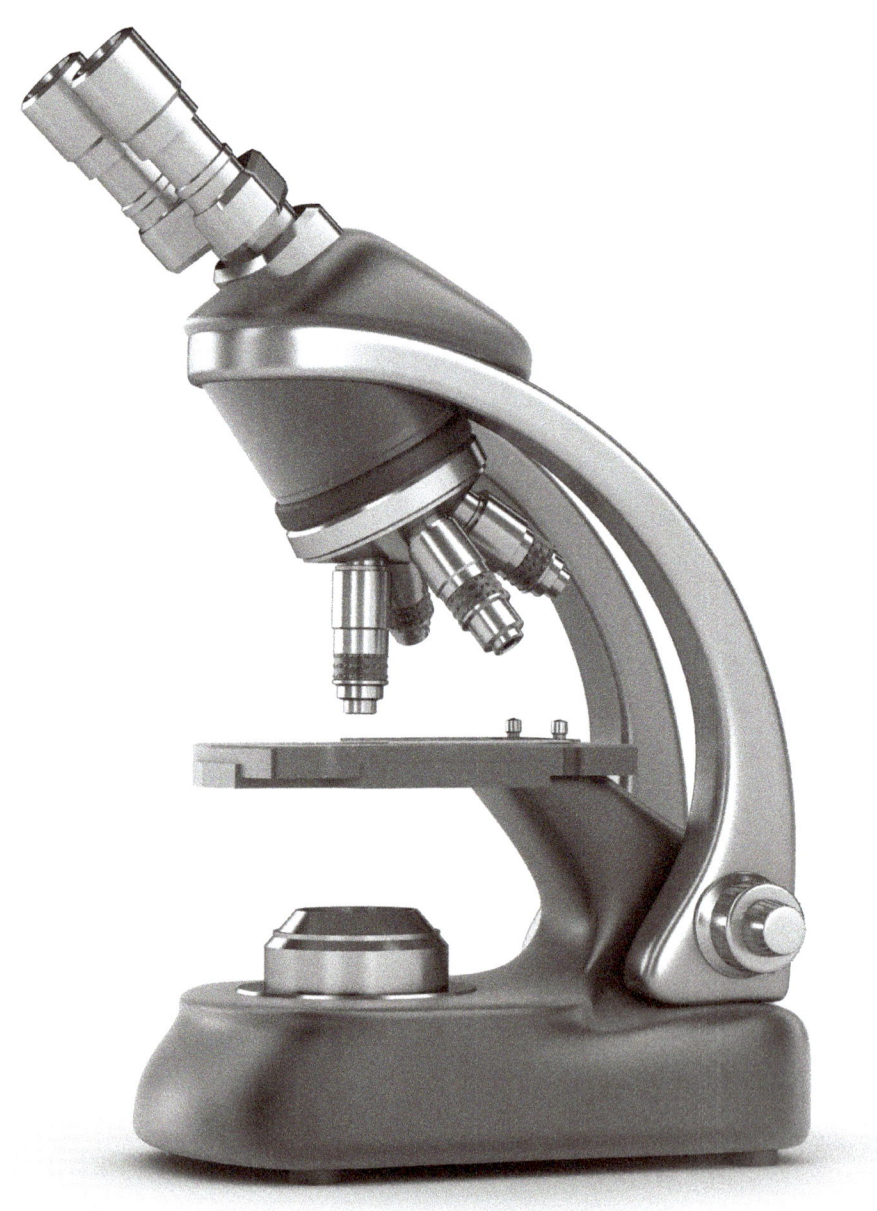

Molécula

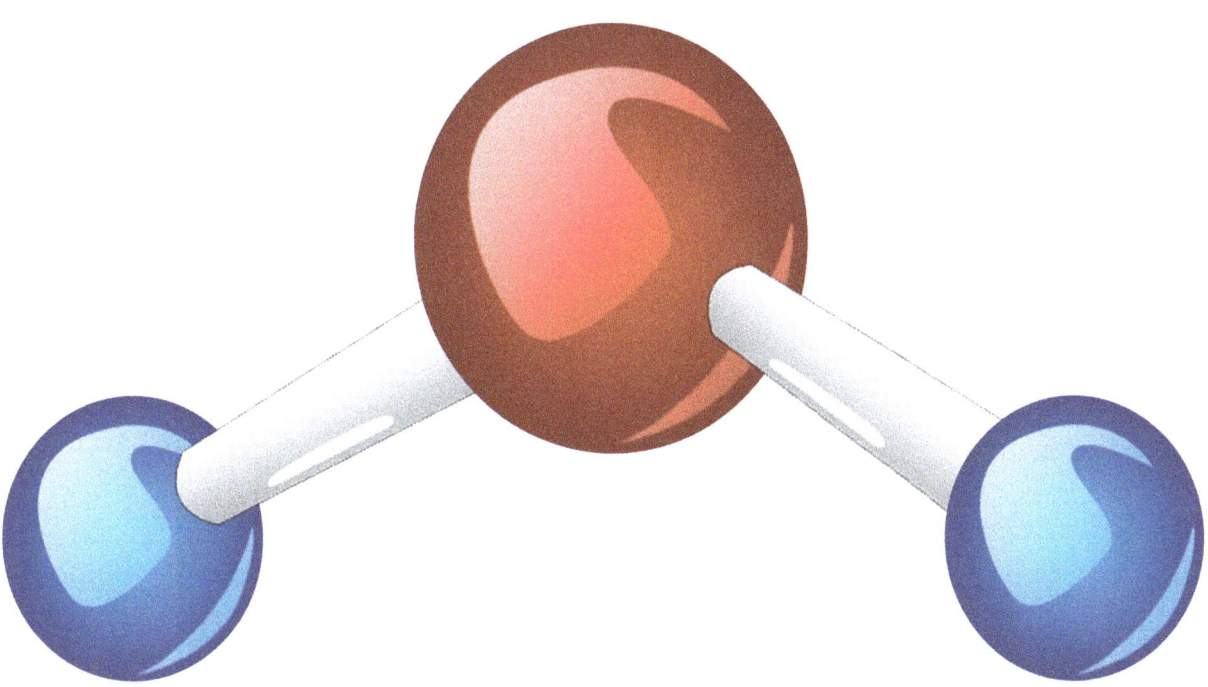

Tabla periódica de elementos

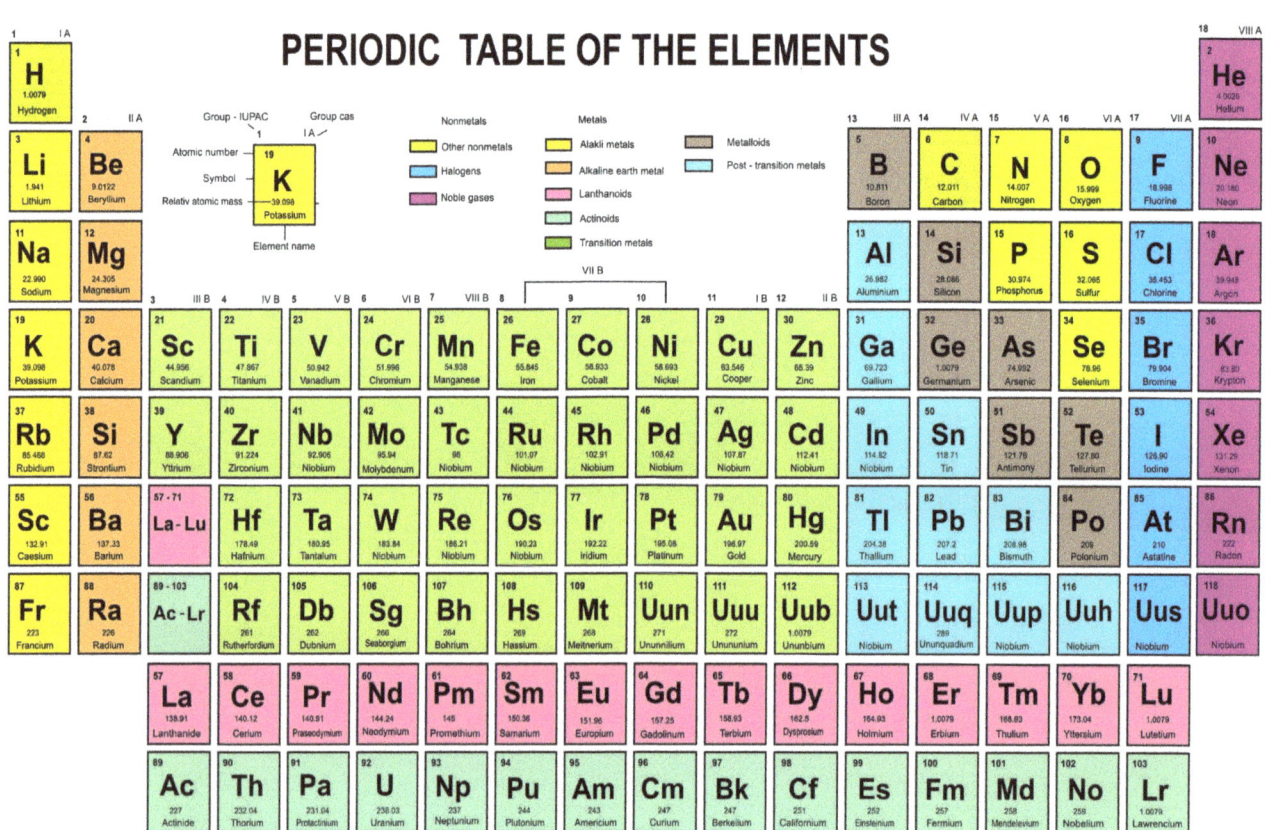

Plato de petri

Robot

Gafas de seguridad

Científico

Guantes estériles

Tubos quirúrgicos

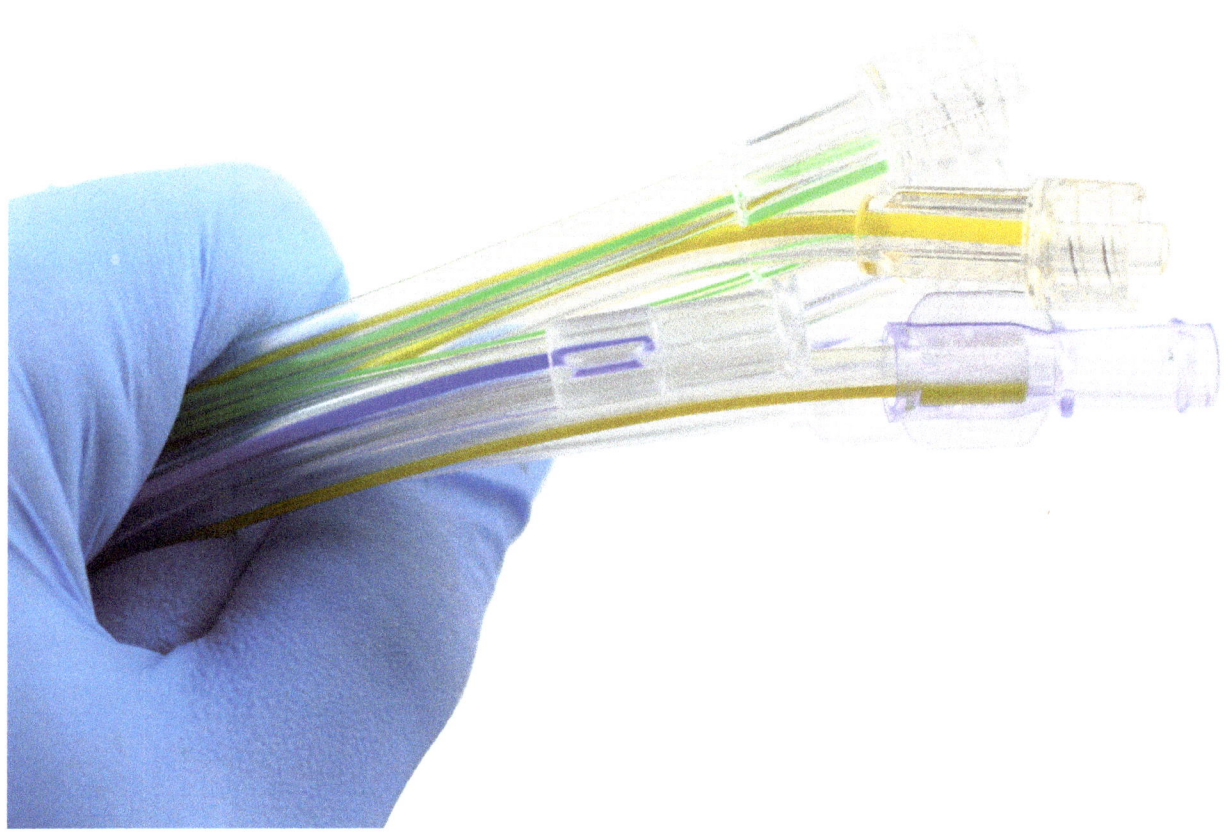

Jeringa y viales

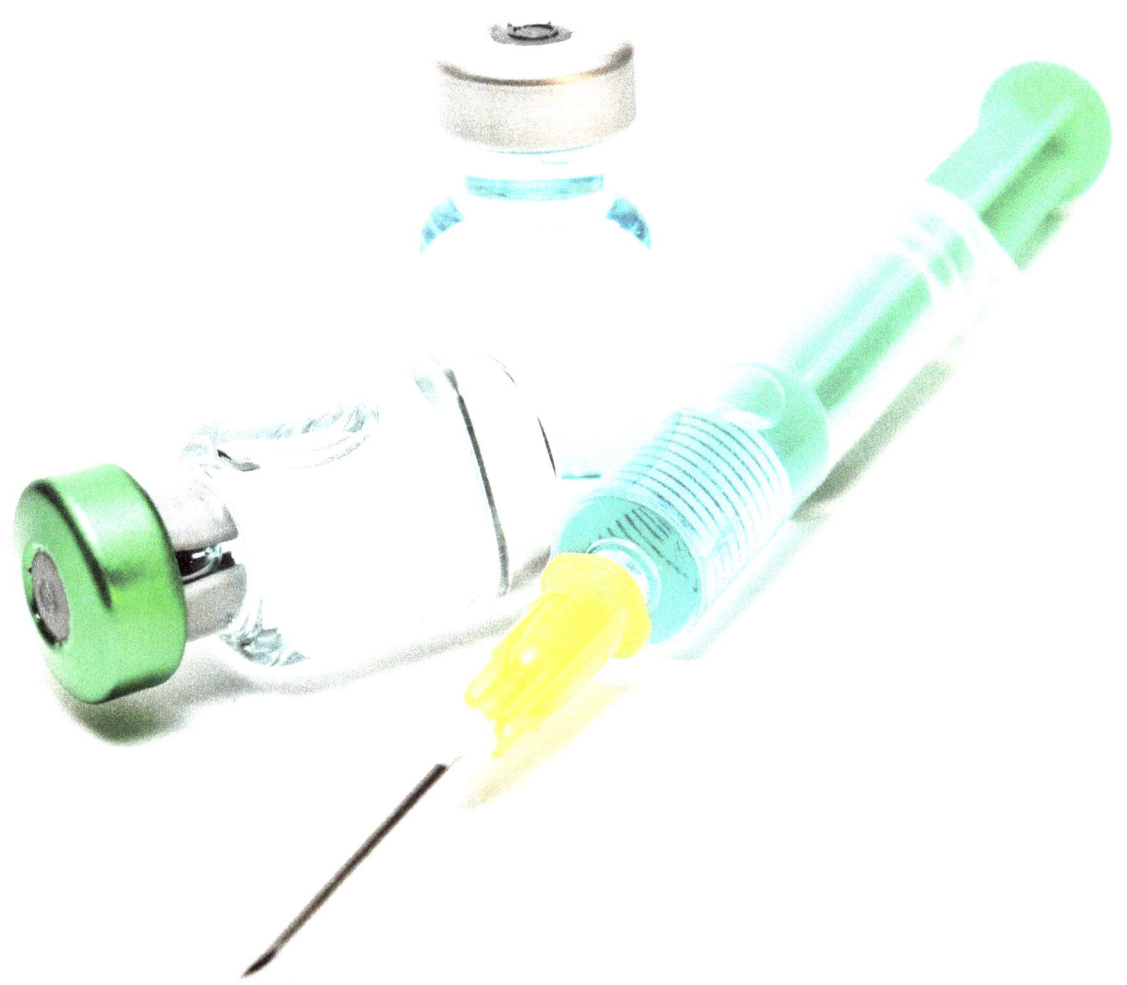

Equipo de científicos

Viales

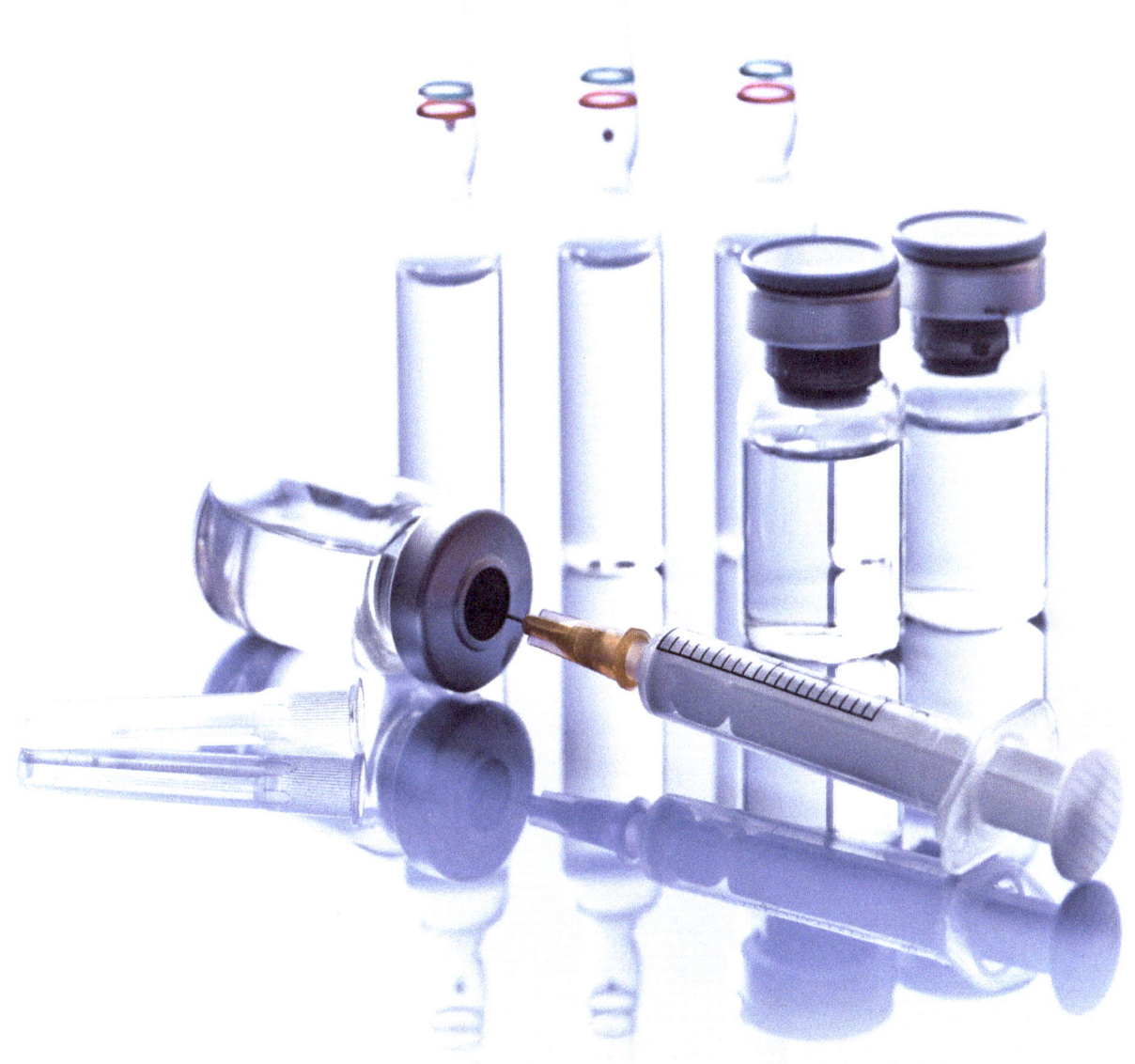

Make Sure to Check Out the Other Discover Series Books from Xist Publishing:

Published in the United States by Xist Publishing
www.xistpublishing.com
PO Box 61593 Irvine, CA 92602

© 2018 by Xist Publishing All rights reserved
Translated by Lenny Sandoval
No portion of this book may be reproduced without express permission of the publisher
All images licensed from Fotolia
First Spanish Edition

ISBN: 978-1-5324-0778-9   eISBN: 978-1-5324-0779-6

xist Publishing

www.ingramcontent.com/pod-product-compliance
Lightning Source LLC
LaVergne TN
LVHW070950070426
835507LV00030B/3476